COMBAT USE OF THE

DOUBLE EDGED

FIGHTING KNIFE

MW01138073

COMBAT USE OF THE

DOUBLE-EDGED

FIGHTING KNIFE

COL. REX APPLEGATE

PALADIN PRESS • BOULDER, COLORADO

Also by Col. Rex Applegate:
Kill or Get Killed
Riot Control: Materiel and Techniques
Scouting and Patrolling: Ground Reconnaissance Principles and Training

Combat Use of the Double-Edged Fighting Knife
by Col. Rex Applegate

Copyright © 1993 by Col. Rex Applegate

ISBN 0-87364-735-1
Printed in the United States of America

Published by Paladin Press, a division of
Paladin Enterprises, Inc., P.O. Box 1307,
Boulder, Colorado 80306, USA.
(303) 443-7250

Direct inquiries and/or orders to the above address.

All rights reserved. Except for use in a review, no
portion of this book may be reproduced in any form
without the express written permission of the publisher.

Neither the author nor the publisher assumes
any responsibility for the use or misuse of
information contained in this book.

CONTENTS

WARNING

This book is *for information purposes only*. It is *not* a training manual. The techniques and drills depicted in this book are extremely dangerous. Do not attempt any of these techniques and drills without proper professional supervision and training. Attempting to do so can result in severe injury or death.

The author and the publisher expressly disclaim any liability from any damage or injuries that a user of this book may suffer. The author and the publisher expressly disclaim any liability from any damage or injuries to third parties from the user of this book.

INTRODUCTION

Training in knife fighting as a specific skill was first introduced during World War II. It was first taught to the British Commandos and other Allied special forces. Later, Office of Strategic Services (OSS) personnel, U.S. Army Rangers, U.S. Marine Corps Raiders, airborne troops, and other elite American units received such instruction. The knife-fighting techniques advocated were generally based on the methods described in the books *Get Tough* (W.E. Fairbairn, 1942) and *Kill or Get Killed* (Rex Applegate, 1943), covering the combat use of the Fairbairn-Sykes Commando knife.

After training and close association with both W.E. Fairbairn and E.A. Sykes while assigned to the OSS in 1943, this writer was ordered to duty at the U.S. Army Military Intelligence Training Center at Camp Ritchie, Maryland. The purpose of the assignment was to organize and direct the Combat Section of this new center, where intensive close-quarter armed and unarmed combat instruction was the training mission. Over the ensuing two years, approximately ten thousand trainees from all walks of life and with many foreign language capabilities were processed there. During this time my instructional staff and I were exposed to trainees who, because of their various ethnic backgrounds, had a great deal of experience in use of the knife as a primary fighting instrument. We evaluated practically all of the world's knife-fighting

1

Col. Rex Applegate is universally recognized as one of the foremost authorities on close-combat with or without weapons. His three books are used worldwide by military and police. Kill or Get Killed *is the best-selling book on close-combat in history.* Riot Control *and* Scouting and Patrolling *are acclaimed as the basic texts on the subjects.*

techniques with single- and double-edged blades; however, nothing evolved superior to the basic Fairbairn-Sykes technique with the double-edgedd knife.

Currently, there are a number of commercially available double-edged knives that the modern student of knife fighting can employ in the manner to be discussed. Their effectiveness depends on blade design, balance, handle shape, etc., as well as the skill of the user. The Randall #2, the Gerber Mark I and II (with variations), the Kershaw Trooper, the Al Mar Shadow, the Applegate-Fairbairn (A-F) models, some EK models, and similar types fall in this category. U.S. Army Trench Knife M3 and bayonets M4, 5, 6, and 7 can all be used to a lesser degree in the system to follow.

This writer favors the current custom and commercial models of the A-F for stated, practical, and combat-proven reasons.

SCOPE AND ORIENTATION

The purpose of this manual is to outline proper use, in close-quarter combat, of a knife specifically designed for that purpose. Basic information is presented to instill confidence and provide skill in the use of the double-edged knife.

A properly trained knife fighter armed with a double-edged knife should prevail in any close-quarter encounters against individuals armed with most weapons, other than firearms. In fact, at close quarters, given the element of surprise, the opponent armed with a handgun is still vulnerable to deadly attacks against a trained knife fighter. "One-on-one" knife-fighting incidents—where both men are forewarned, similarly armed, and engaged—are extremely rare. Generally, knife confrontations should be over in seconds when the trained knife fighter is pitted against an untrained, or unprepared, opponent—especially when the element of surprise is present.

THE KNIFE BLADE
AND HANDLE

The heart of the fighting knife is its blade. It should be 5 to 7 inches in length, double-edged, and wide enough to be razor sharp on both sides all the way back to the cross guard. The point must be sharp enough to penetrate and thick and tough enough to withstand side pressure.

The blade should provide slashing, ripping, and thrusting capabilities. Stainless type steel, correctly tempered, with a dull finish is preferable. The blade should be tempered to hold an edge, as well as being easily sharpened and, at the same time, not brittle.

The oval-shape handle should fit the palm of the hand and be designed so that the edges of the blade can be immediately, and automatically, located in dark or light conditions. A nonslip surface is another feature that should be incorporated. The handle should not turn in the hand (sweaty palms, etc.) when the blade strikes resistance. The knife should be handle heavy with relation to balance. Nothing in the design should limit its possibilities for use as a weapon from any position or either hand. The overall length should be approximately 10 to 11 inches; anything longer makes it too unwieldy and cumbersome to carry. The weight should be in the 1/2 to 3/4 pound range.

CORRECT GRIP

A.   The handle of the knife lies diagonally across the palm of the holding hand. The blade extends from the thumb side, the handle end from the little finger side.

B.   The thumb and index finger tightly grasp the handle in the area nearest the cross guard. The tip of the thumb is wedged against the guard, as is the first point of the index finger, which is curled around the handle beneath the thumb.

C.   The remaining fingers lie over the handle in a natural fashion; the second finger lies over the largest diameter of the oval handle. The ring finger lies behind the second finger, and the little finger lies over the handle's smallest diameter, near the pommel.

D.   The weapon's point of balance is back from the guard, under the index finger. The knife is controlled by the thumb and index finger and by turning the wrist (palm up or down), depending on the slashing stroke to be used. Like tennis, the palm is down for a backhand stroke, or slash, and up for a forehand. This type of grip is essential to proper employment of the knife in combat. At the time of contact with the opponent, all fingers grip the handle tightly. Used with this fencing foil-type grip, the knife becomes an extension of the hand, not an appendage.

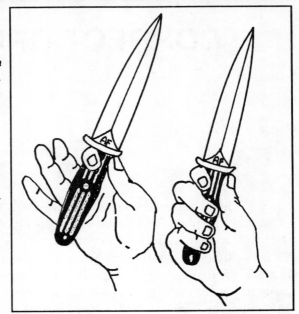

The correct fencing-foil, across-the-palm-type grip when one is using a double-edged fighting knife. Grasped in this manner, the knife becomes an extension of the hand. By turning the wrist, thrusts, forehand and backhand slashes, and ripping strokes are possible. This grip works with either hand.

VARIOUS KNIFE GRIPS

A.   The ice-pick grip is often used when the knife is grasped by an unskilled person. The handle is grasped tightly in the fist, with the blade extending downward from the little finger side of the hand. The basic offensive movement is limited to a downward stabbing motion or upward slash, for which there are several effective defenses.

B.   The hammer grip is characterized by gripping the handle in the manner of a hammer handle, with the blade extending upward from the thumb side of the hand. Offensive movement is confined to an upward thrust or downward slash, which is relatively simple to block or parry.

C.   The razor grip, popularized in the movies, is typically employed as a surprise slashing attack by a semiskilled person. It is a popular one for use with a single-edge knife or razor.

TOP: The ice pick-type grip

CENTER: The hammer type.

BOTTOM: Razor grip with single edge protruding from little finger side of hand, with blade parallel to forearm.

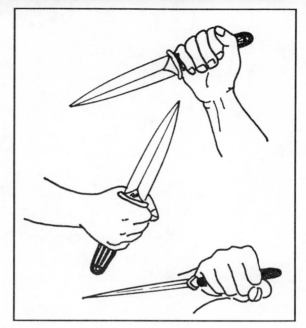

The handle is turned down, and the blade protrudes from the finger side of the palm, edge forward. The blade is held parallel to the arm, etc. Offensive movement is confined to horizontal slashes, and a return thrust may be executed. The entire basic stroke can be blocked.

All the above grips are commonly used by unskilled (or a few semiskilled) persons, generally using a single-edged knife. Their basic weakness is that they require the knife wielder to get *extremely close* to the opponent, where various blocks, parries, disarming methods, and offensive counter-measures can be employed against the user.

STANCE

A correct stance, using the double-edged blade, allows for rapid movement, maneuverability, and attack, while keeping the opponent at a distance.

A. Holding the head erect, drop into a balanced crouch with the knees flexed, feet about shoulder-width apart, and one foot advanced in front of the other. Your center of gravity should be in the stomach-abdomen area, which is the most vulnerable area to protect from your opponent's blade.

B. Using the correct grip, hold the knife hand close to your body at waist level.

C. The free hand should be extended slightly in front, at a level between the waist and knee, while in a crouch. Shoulders should be lowered, in a relaxed position, and with the free-hand shoulder slightly ahead of the other.

D. The correct stance keeps your knife hand well out of your opponent's reach and allows the free hand to make feints or parries, misdirect the opponent's eyes, or throw objects to disconcert the enemy. This protects the vulnerable midsection and puts you in a position to move to meet any type of attack or counter any defense.

The knife fighter viewed from the front. The free hand can be used to throw objects into adversaries' eyes, make distracting movements, and fend off, or parry, defensive action or attacks with a weapon used by the opponent.

The correct way to carry the knife from an aggressive forward crouch. The feet should be placed one in front of the other in a position whereby balance is always maintained and the body position can be changed in any direction by foot movement.

KNIFE MANIPULATIONS

A.   By using the correct stance, you are able to direct slashes to the adversary's face, neck, hands, and legs with a double-edged, razor-sharp knife. Disabling slashes to the tendons of the inside of the wrists and back of the hands are very effective.

B.   Using the correct stance and grip, effective thrusts can be made to the throat, trunk, stomach, groin, or heart. Deep cuts, slashes, and thrusts to the heart area and throat usually are immediately fatal. *When practicing, get into the habit of executing a "ripping" motion as you withdraw from a thrust to a vital area.*

C.   The best thrusting method is to move forward and pivot on your forward leg, while simultaneously snapping your blade forward at the same time your opposite leg, shoulder, and arm move backward, etc.

A slash to the back of the hand will sever tendons so that control of the fingers will be lost.

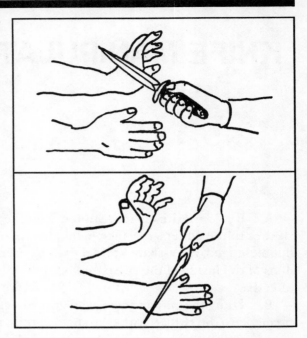

TACTICS

A.   Always use surprise, if possible, in your attack.

B.   Many times a scream, yell, or battle cry accompanied by a surprise attack will so destroy your enemy's *mental balance* that he will be disabled, or dead, before he has a chance to react.

C.   Use your free hand to create movement, diverting the enemy's eyes from your knife hand. Use feints; throw handfuls of dirt, gravel, coins, etc., into his face; or try some similar ruse.

D.   Coupled with feints involving the free hand, constantly make continuous false moves with your knife hand from the throat to knee area and then follow up with a slash to the arm, wrist, face, and throat. For example, a slash across the forehead will instantly cause a flow of blood to blind your opponent, etc.

E.   Generally disabling slashes to the wrist, biceps, etc., are real building blocks to finishing off with a well-placed thrust.

VULNERABLE POINTS

Studies conducted by law enforcement agencies show that approximately 50 percent of all fatal knife attacks involve multiple thrusts to the trunk area, while almost 40 percent involve the head and neck area. Generally speaking, thrusts are more effective than slashes in causing death. Slashes, however, are the real "stepping-stones" of knife fighting. Slashes and cuts to the hands, wrists, and forearms disable and demoralize your enemy to the point that you can finish him off with a well-placed thrust to vital areas.

ARTERIES

A.   Study the accompanying diagram carefully. The approximate positions of vulnerable arteries are given. A strike to any one of them will cause unconsciousness within two to 30 seconds and death in a maximum of two minutes. Remember the position of each; do not worry if you cannot remember the names.

B.   Following is a list of vulnerable points where knife wounds will be particularly effective.

HEAD AND NECK AREAS

A.   Base of skull (thrust)

No.	Name of Artery	Size	Depth below Surface in inches	Loss of Consciousness in seconds	Death	
1....	Brachial	Medium	½	14	1½	Min.
2....	Radial	Small	¼	30	2	"
3....	Carotid	Large	1½	5	12	Sec.
4....	Subclavian	Large	2½	2	3½	"
5....	(Heart)	——	3½	Instantaneous	3	"
6....	(Stomach)	—·—	5	Depending on depth of cut		

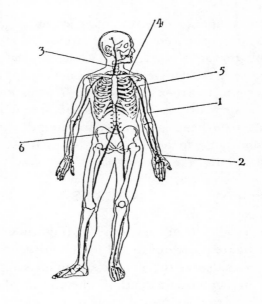

This diagram from W.E. Fairbairn's Get Tough *shows vulnerable arteries, varying in size from a thumb to a pencil in diameter. Thrusts to the heart and slashes to the throat are the most deadly strokes. The psychological and shock effect of a thrust or slash to the stomach-groin area is very effective and usually will cause the recipient to lose his mental balance and control, even though it is not immediately fatal.*

18

B. Temple (thrust)
C. Eyes and forehead (thrust or slash)
D. Mouth (thrust or slash)
E. Side of neck (slash)
F. Beneath chin (thrust or slash)
G. Base of throat (thrust)

TRUNK

A. Heart (thrust)
B. Stomach (thrust, slash, rip)
C. Kidney (thrust, rip)
D. Groin, abdomen, stomach (thrust, slash, rip)

LIMBS

A. Biceps (slash)
B. Forearm (slash)
C. Wrist (inside slash)
D. Back of hand, fingers (slash)
E. Thigh (inside slash)

UTILITY KNIVES—
KNIFE THROWING

Although, single-edged utility knives can be used for combat, they are less suitable. They are designed to be of more service in dressing game or performing routine camp cutting chores, etc. Although you can use any double-edged fighting knife for noncombat purposes, it is best to carry an additional utility single-edged knife such as a Kabar.

Knife throwing is for the circus or vaudeville stage. To throw a knife so it will strike point-first, you must know the *exact distance* to accurately predict the number of revolutions the knife will make as it revolves through the air. Throwing a knife under conditions of combat and stress is not advised and will probably only result in loss of the weapon.

KNIFE MAINTENANCE

SHARPENING

A.   Fighting blades require a keen edge, sharpened on a good-quality natural or synthetic sharpening stone. A double-faced stone with both medium and fine grits is ideal. In the field, use water or saliva to lubricate your sharpening stone. However, light machine oil is the best stone lubricant.

B.   Blade edges are maintained at an approximate 15- to 20-degree angle. A greater angle will be too blunt and will dull quickly; a lesser angle will be too thin and is prone to chipping.

C.   In order to give your blade the require edge, proceed as follows:

1. Lubricate your stone with water or oil and place one flat of the blade against the surface of the stone.
2. Tilt the center of the blade up 1/16 of an inch, as if you were about to slice away a thin film from the stone's surface.
3. Sweep the edge of the blade off the stone from heel to point. Use an even, steady stroke and maintain your angle.
4. There are numerous sharpening devices on the market that enable correct sharpening of angles to be maintained.
5. Turn the blade over and repeat the operation. Sharpen by alternating sides equally.
6. Finish by stropping the blade on the heel of your hand, your leather scabbard, or belt.

RUST PREVENTION

Although most modern blades are made from so-called "stainless steel," cleanliness is still your best protection against rust or corrosion. Never allow blood to dry on your blade, and be certain to wipe and oil the blade after use. Do not store your blade in a leather scabbard for long periods of time. Certain chemicals used in the tanning process may cause corrosion.

PRACTICE

Although knife-against-knife encounters are extremely rare, two-man "one-on-one" practice with rubber knives and protective goggles is still recommended. Edges of the knives can be coated with chalk or old lipstick to leave marks so as to create realism.

Another practicing technique is to construct a cutting tree

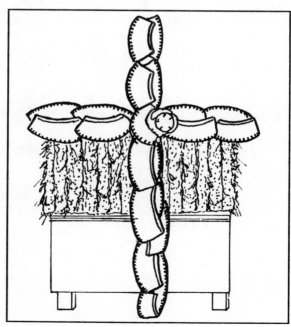

A cutting tree used for training. It is a 4-inch pole covered with cut-up sections of automobile tires; a bale of hay, cotton, rags, or other material is placed in back. Cuts, thrusts, and slashes (always followed up by a ripping motion on withdrawal) should be practiced until they are instinctive and automatic.

25

from old tire casings. This proved to be a useful device in training during World War II.

KNIFE DEFENSE

Against the type of knife fighting and manipulation described in this text, conventional knife defenses—as taught in most police academies, martial arts schools, and military installations—are generally unsatisfactory. Only the most skilled, highly trained individuals can successfully prevail in unarmed encounters in one-on-one situations. The best defenses are: run; shoot; or use a baton, club, chair, or other improvised weapon.

One of the best police-training videos is *Surviving Edged Weapons* from Calibre Press. This video should be shown to all serious knife-fighting trainees. It is significant that no practical unarmed defense in this training tape is advocated against the techniques described herein.

SHEATH

    The sheath should be made of a quality, thick, or tanned leather that will keep its shape (not warping) after continuous field use. Leather conditioner should be used when necessary. Sheaths made of plastic or other man-made materials are also acceptable. A good fighting knife demands a quality sheath.

COMBAT USE OF THE DOUBLE-EDGED FIGHTING KNIFE

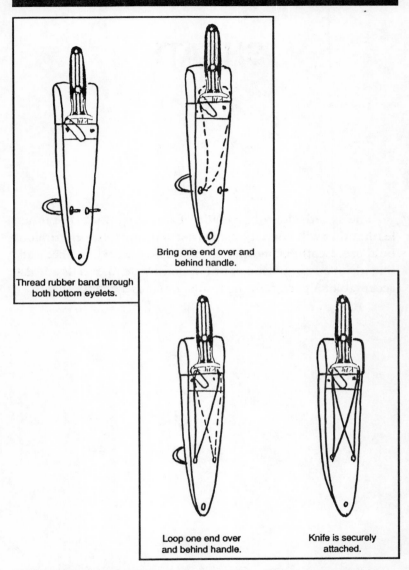

Thread rubber band through both bottom eyelets.

Bring one end over and behind handle.

Loop one end over and behind handle.

Knife is securely attached.

It is the practice among paratroopers to tie their knives in a handle-down position prior to jumping. Due to an accident or a faulty retaining strap or snap, often the knife is lost on impact with the ground. The above method, using the hollow, tubular grommets in the sheath, provides insurance against knife loss and still permits the knife to be withdrawn by breaking the rubber band (or string) at the time of removal.

A razor-sharp, dou-ble-edged knife can be dangerous to the user, particular-ly when inserting in the sheath off the belt. Even when hanging on the belt, care and time should be taken to insert the blade point. Leather sheaths that have been exposed to the elements (becoming wet and then dry) can lose their shapes and sometimes warp.

Off the belt, do not hold the sheath in the palm of the hand when insert-ing the knife. Hook the thumb in the belt loop as illus-trated above.

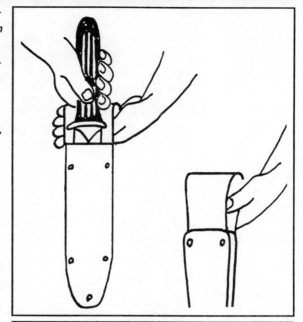

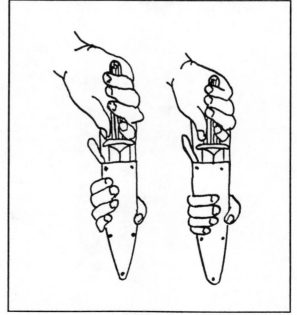

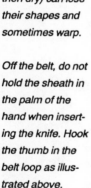

HISTORY OF THE APPLEGATE– FAIRBAIRN KNIFE

The A-F fighting knife is a double-edged weapon designed primarily for combat use. Any utility value it may have is secondary. It is the only fighting knife ever designed based on extensive after-action combat reports that took place during World War II, when thousands of men were trained with and used the Fairbairn-Sykes (F-S) Knife, designed by E.A. Sykes and W.E. Fairbairn of Shanghai police and British commando fame.

The original F-S was popularly known as "The Commando Knife" or dagger. It became the most famous fighting knife design in history, and it was issued by British Ordnance and later by the American OSS. Crossed Commando knives appeared on various shoulder patches and insignia, becoming symbols of the victorious Allied war effort over the Axis forces.

As World War II progressed, many negative combat reports began to accumulate regarding the original F-S, which was at that time being manufactured by a number of British firms whose attention to quality of blade materials and adherence to the original design (by Wilkinson Sword) were poorly executed.

Reports from the battlefront indicated that the knives were not only being misused by the troops for utility purposes, but were also too weak in the blade, breaking at the tip and at the cross guard.

It was almost impossible to sharpen them to get a good cutting edge because of the narrow width and thickness of the

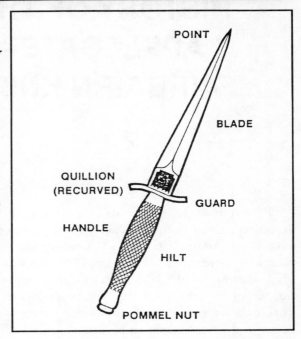

The first pattern Fairbairn-Sykes Commando dagger manufactured by Wilkinson Sword. Later models issued by British Ordnance were of slightly different blade and handle configuration and below earlier quality standards.

POINT

BLADE

QUILLION (RECURVED)

GUARD

HANDLE

HILT

POMMEL NUT

blade and sharp angle of the grind. The Coke-bottle-shaped handle permitted slippage.

Not only was the round handle too small for many hands, it also did not allow (especially at night) for the user to be able to instantly locate, by "feel," the blade's edge. Some reports actually came back where men had tried to cut the throats of enemy sentries with the flat of the blade.

In late 1943, W.E. Fairbairn and this writer redesigned the knife to correct the problems being encountered on the battlefield. The blade was widened, strengthened, and redesigned to hold an edge, the tang strengthened, and the handle made more oval. In 1944, a prototype was produced that corrected most of the combat faults that had become evident. Unfortunately, by that time the pace of the war had increased and the priorities were such that the prototype was never put into production.

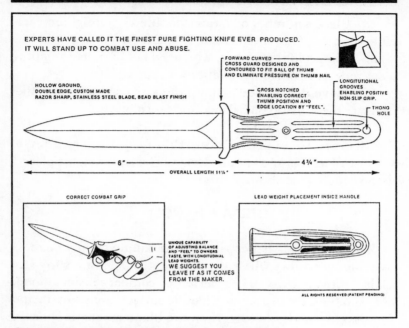

EXPERTS HAVE CALLED IT THE FINEST PURE FIGHTING KNIFE EVER PRODUCED.
IT WILL STAND UP TO COMBAT USE AND ABUSE.

FORWARD CURVED
CROSS GUARD DESIGNED AND
CONTOURED TO FIT BALL OF THUMB
AND ELIMINATE PRESSURE ON THUMB NAIL

HOLLOW GROUND,
DOUBLE EDGE, CUSTOM MADE
RAZOR SHARP, STAINLESS STEEL BLADE, BEAD BLAST FINISH

CROSS NOTCHED
ENABLING CORRECT
THUMB POSITION AND
EDGE LOCATION BY "FEEL".

LONGITUTIONAL
GROOVES
ENABLING POSITIVE
NON-SLIP GRIP.

THONG
HOLE

6"

4¾"

OVERALL LENGTH 11¼"

CORRECT COMBAT GRIP

LEAD WEIGHT PLACEMENT INSIDE HANDLE

UNIQUE CAPABILITY
OF ADJUSTING BALANCE
AND "FEEL" TO OWNERS
TASTE, WITH LONGITUDINAL
LEAD WEIGHTS.
WE SUGGEST YOU
LEAVE IT AS IT COMES
FROM THE MAKER.

ALL RIGHTS RESERVED (PATENT PENDING)

Special features of the Applegate-Fairbairn Fighting Knife.

This writer retained the original prototype knife, along with the original drawings. Renewed interest in fighting knives prompted the introduction in 1983 of a relatively inexpensive custom-made version of the A-F Knife. This model is still available, and more than a thousand of these custom knives have now been sold to collectors and members of special elite military units.

BALANCE

Baseball players have favorite bats; golfers prefer certain clubs. Likewise, the balance and "feel" of any double-edged fighting knife is an important psychological element in the selection of a make or model. This important factor is very evident when the A-F Knife is selected over other types. A simple test emphasizes this point.

35

1.   Place a number of various double-edged fighters on a table (Randall, Gerber, Kershaw, A-F, Ek, etc.)
2.   Blindfold the trainee, who need not have had any previous indoctrination or familiarity with such knives.
3.   Have the trainee pick up the knives one by one and evaluate them based on balance and feel alone.

Chances are overwhelming that he will pick the A-F because of its feel and handle design. The lead weights placed in the handle contribute to this selection.

THE A-F HANDLE

The long, oval-shape, palm-filling handle greatly increases maneuverability when gripped tightly. The "no-slip" factor is critical. Sweaty palms caused by combat tension, blood, etc., combined with a smooth handle surface, are a sure recipe for disaster and knife loss when the blade meets resistance. The A-F Knife handle is made of molded plastic (Lexan™), thereby permitting the addition of the deep, longitudinal grooves and balance-influencing lead weights. A hard, combat-induced hand grip forces the flesh of the palm into the grooves, forming a secure bond between the hand and knife under combat conditions.

A commercial model of the A-F Knife is now being offered to the public at a greatly reduced price with no appreciable sacrifice in quality. It is hoped that more of the world's fighting men will be able to take advantage of the A-F Knife, now proven on the world's battlefields.

SOURCES FOR KNIVES, BOOKS, AND VIDEOS

BOOKS

Get Tough
Kill or Get Killed

Publisher: Paladin Press
Box 1307
Boulder, CO 80306
303-443-7250

KNIVES

Applegate-Fairbairn Knife (Commercial Model)

Manufacturer: Blackjack Knives Ltd.
1307 W. Wabash Avenue
Effingham, IL 62401
217-347-7700

MAIL-ORDER

Knives
A-F Custom Model (made by William Harsey)
A-F Commercial Model (Blackjack Knives)
A-F Rubber Training Knives (Al Mar type)

COMBAT USE OF THE DOUBLE-EDGED FIGHTING KNIFE

Books and Video
Combat Use of the Double-Edged Fighting Knife
Get Tough
Kill or Get Killed
Surviving Edged Weapons (Calibre Press, VHS,
  approximately 85 min.)

Supplier: Wells Creek Knife and Gun Works
32956 State Highway 38
Scottsburg, OR 97473
503-587-4202